DESIGN AND MAKE
CUSHIONS
HEATHER LUKE

NEW HOLLAND

For Don

———————

First published in 1996 by
New Holland (Publishers) Ltd
London • Cape Town • Sydney • Singapore

24 Nutford Place
London W1H 6DQ
United Kingdom

80 McKenzie Street
Cape Town 8001
South Africa

3/2 Aquatic Drive
Frenchs Forest, NSW 2086
Australia

Reprinted 1996

ISBN 1 85368 530 5 (hbk)
ISBN 1 85368 531 3 (pbk)

Managing Editor: Gillian Haslam
Editor: Coral Walker
Designer: Kit Johnson
Photographer: David Johnson
Illustrations: Lizzie Sanders

Typeset by Ace Filmsetting Ltd, Frome, Somerset

Reproduction by Hirt and Carter (Pty) Ltd
Printed and bound in Malaysia by Times Offset (m) sdn Bhd

ACKNOWLEDGEMENTS

With grateful thanks to Sarah Westcott, Julie Toop and Jackie Pullman for their expert
help; to David Johnson for the lovely photographs; to Yvonne McFarlane, Gillian
Haslam, Coral Walker and Kit Johnson for bringing the pieces together.
Elizabeth Peck and Jano Clarke allowed me to photograph their lovely homes and
capture some 'cushioned corners'. Thank you.

CONTENTS

INTRODUCTION

One single cushion in an unusual fabric with striking colour combinations can be all that is needed and could be made by even the most reluctant seamstress.

Style is a word which is open to many interpretations and indeed is interpreted differently by each of us. However, when it is present, style is instantly recognisable. Whether our home is a country mansion or an apartment in a large city; whether the architecture is beautiful and inspiring, or whether there is little inherent form and character to the dwelling, we each need to consider and choose a style for our furnishings.

Each of us is interested in their own home and I find that even when the skills or time are not available for making the curtains, covers and larger soft furnishings, most of us like to make some cushions. Although making the cushions does appear to be the easiest task, the importance of choosing the accessories - including pictures and lamps - gives the opportunity for a completely individual finish to each room.

A country-inspired interior will call for simplicity, rough textures, and practicality. Mixing fabrics - checks with florals and stripes, crunchy cottons and linens with wool tweeds - immediately offers the desired informality and practicality. A sophisticated town house will call for elegance, embellishment and detailed, but understated, design. Silks, satins and sheers, the finest worked and woven linens, tonal mixes of similar fabrics and fine handwork bring quality to the fore.

DESIGN AND MAKE CUSHIONS

This book has been designed so that even the beginner should be able confidently and successfully to tackle their first project. Always start with something that is well within your own capabilities. Much better a simple but well made scatter cushion in the right fabric and situation, with the corners square and the pattern well placed than a mountain of complicated but poorly finished covers. Enjoy the result of your efforts and then try another, until you have gained confidence.

Even if you find sewing a chore, I hope that this book will give you the inspiration and desire to plan interesting cushions for someone else to make up for you.

CHOOSING FABRICS

Cushions offer the opportunity to experiment with different combinations of styles, textures, colours and sizes. Remnants and offcuts from previous projects, from travels abroad or bought on impulse will come into their own sooner or later. Fold your fabric over a cushion pad and try it in even the most unlikely places.

Cushion covers should always be made with great attention to detail, not obvious until closely examined, such as the subtlety of a piping colour, the tone and size of a tassel or the position of a button. Mixing fabrics and colours for cushions to accessorise sofas and beds can be great fun and can involve many and varied fabric types.

I almost never plan all of the cushions in a scheme so that I give myself the chance of adding or subtracting, emphasising or playing down a colour or fabric

once most of the furnishings are together and I can actually see the setting. Sometimes just an extra texture or change of size and scale is needed.

Always try the seemingly obvious and consider the seemingly opposite. A sofa might

Here, woven damask, printed linens, silks and cottons combine harmoniously, all very different but with compatible scale and tonal grouping, picking up the colours from the walls, the sofa and the wool throw.

need seven medium-sized cushions or three very large ones; they might need to be in a mixture of colours, textures and fabrics or all in the same. Should there be detailed and extravagant trimmings, or none at all?

Cushions can be changed with the seasons. You might like to have wools and tweeds in rich colours in the winter, changing to light chintzes or pastel silks for the summer. If your sofa and chair covers are plain and simple, the scope for cushion fabrics will be even greater.

All white makes its own timeless statement (above right). New pillows and covers which have been chosen for washable practicality set off the beautifully hand-worked 19th century cotton and lace covers which need to be protected from regular laundering if they are to be handed down to the next generation. If you take the time to look in antique shops and markets, you should be able to find Victorian pillows, cushions, tablecloths and nightdress cases in very good condition. The best buys are those which have been completely hand stitched, perhaps even with handmade lace and buttons. Modern whitework from the Far East is also often hand stitched but the work is not as fine as that from the last century.

Cushions need to be in keeping with the character of the house and the decorative style chosen. Tapestries worked in muted colours (right) sit on antique velvet upholstered chairs, and with 'bashed-out' hand printed linen curtains and antique furnishings, they form just one part of the whole, very appealing, setting.

BASIC TECHNIQUES

STITCHES

Start and finish all stitching with a double stitch; never use a knot.

Hemming stitch

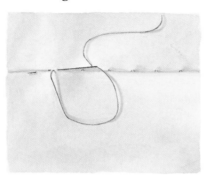

This stitch is used for hems. Each stitch should be approximately 1.5 cm (⅝ in) in length. Slide the needle through the folded hem, pick up two threads of the main fabric, and push the needle directly back into the fold.

Herringbone stitch

Use over any raw edge which is then covered by another fabric. This stitch is worked in the opposite direction to all other

stitches, so right handers will work from left to right. Each stitch should be approximately 3 cm (1¼ in). Stitch into the hem, from right to left; about 1.5 cm (⅝ in) to the right make a stitch into the curtain picking up two threads. Pull through and stitch 1.5 cm (⅝ in) to the right making a stitch into the hem.

Ladder stitch

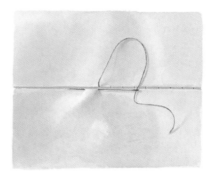

Ladder stitch is used to join two folded edges invisibly together. Slide the needle along the fold 5 mm (¼ in) and straight into the fold opposite. Slide along for 5 mm (¼ in) and back into the first fold, again directly opposite.

Slip stitch

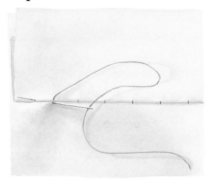

Slide the needle through the fold by 1.5 cm (⅝ in) and pick up two threads of the opposite fabric. Push the needle back into the main fabric exactly opposite and slide through a further 1.5 cm (⅝ in).

Buttonhole stitch

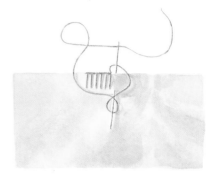

Use to strengthen or neaten a raw edge. Work from left to right with the raw edge uppermost. Push the needle from the back to the front approximately 3 mm (⅛ in) below the edge. Twist the thread around the needle and pull the needle through, carefully tightening the thread so that it knots right on the edge of the fabric to form a ridge.

Blanket stitch

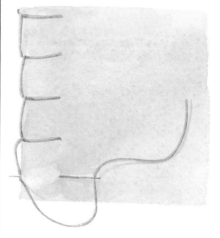

Originally used to neaten the raw edges of woollen blankets, its use is now mainly decorative. It is most comfortable worked from the side with the edge towards you. Push the needle from the front to the back, about 6 mm (¼ in) from the edge (also this measurement will vary with large or small items). Hold the thread from the last stitch under the needle and pull up to make a loop on the edge.

PINNING

When pinning two layers of fabric together or piping on to fabric, always use horizontal and vertical pins to keep the fabric in place. The horizontal pins need to be removed just before the machine foot reaches them and the vertical ones – or cross pins – can remain in place, so the fabrics are held together the whole time.

SEAMS

Flat seam

The most common seam for normal use. With right sides together, pin 1.5–2 cm (⅝–¾ in) in from the edge at 10 cm (4 in) intervals. Pin cross pins halfway between each seam pin. These cross pins will remain in place while you are stitching to prevent the fabrics slipping. Once

machine-stitched, open the seam flat and press from the back. Press from the front. Now press from the back, under each flap to remove the pressed ridge line.

French seam

Use for fine fabrics or when the seam might be visible. Pin the fabrics together with the wrong sides facing. Stitch 5 mm (¼ in) from the raw edges. Trim and flip the fabric over, bringing the right sides together. Pin again, 1 cm (⅜ in) from the stitched edge and stitch along this line to enclose the raw edges. Press from the right side, always pressing the seam in one direction only.

Flat fell seam

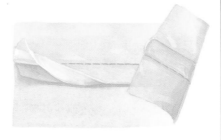

Use for heavier weight fabrics. Pin the fabrics together with the right sides facing and stitch 1.5–3 cm (⅝–1¼ in) from the raw edges. Trim one seam to just under half. Fold the other over to enclose the raw edge. Press down. Stitch close to the fold line.

MAKING TIES

Ties are used throughout soft furnishings. For cushions, they form an attractive and practical feature for tying sides together. They are also the principal means of tying squab cushions to chairs. Headings of curtains and loose covers are other soft furnishings which make use of ties.

Folded ties

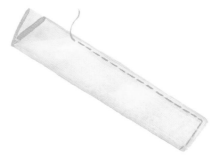

Cut a strip of fabric four times the width of your finished tie and 3 cm (1¼ in) longer.

Press one short end under by 1 cm (⅜ in) and both sides to the middle. Press in half, and stitch close to the fold line.

Rouleau ties

Cut a strip of fabric four times the width of your finished tie and 3 cm (1¼ in) longer. Fold in half lengthwise, right sides together, enclosing a piece of cord which is longer than the strip of fabric. Stitch along the short side to secure the cord firmly. If the rouleau is quite wide, knot the cord as well. Stitch along the length, 2 mm (⅛ in) towards the raw edge from the centre.

Trim the fabric across the corner, pull the cord through, at the same time turning the fabric right side out. Cut off the cord at the end. Press the raw edge under and slipstitch neatly.

PIPING

If piping is to be used in straight lines then it will be easier to handle if cut straight. If it is to be bent around corners, then it should be cut on the cross. For 4 mm (⅛ in) piping cord cut 4 cm (1½ in) wide strips. All joins should be made on the cross to minimise bulk when the fabric is folded.

To cut on the straight
Cut lengths as long as possible. Hold two strips, butting the ends together as if making a continuous length. Trim away both corners at a 45° angle. Hold together and flip the top one over. Stitch where the two pieces cross.

To cut on the cross

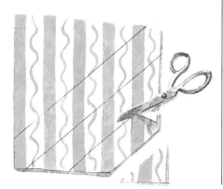

With the fabric flat on the table fold one bottom corner as if making a 30 cm (12 in) square. Cut along the fold line. Mark pencil lines from this cut edge at 4 cm (1½ in) intervals, and cut along these lines. Hold two pieces butting the ends together as if making a continuous strip. Flip the top one over and hold. Stitch together where the two fabrics cross.

Making up

Press seams flat and cut away excess corners. Fold in half along the length and insert the piping cord. Machine stitch to encase, approximately 2 mm (⅛ in) from the cord. Keep the fabric folded exactly in half.

Pinning on
Always pin piping so that the raw edges of the piping line up exactly with the raw edges of the main fabric. The seam allowance is usually 1.5 cm (⅝ in).

To bend piping around curves, snip into the stitching line as often as is necessary for the piping to lie flat. To pipe around a right angle, stop pinning 1.5 cm (⅝ in) from the corner, snip the piping to the stitching line, fold the piping to 90° and start pinning 1.5 cm (⅝ in) on the adjacent side.

Joining
To join piping, overlap by approximately 6 cm (2¼ in) and cut away excess. Unpick the casing on one side and cut away the cord so that the two ends butt up. Fold the piping fabric across at a 45° angle and cut along this fold. Fold under 1 cm (⅜ in) and pin securely before stitching.

BINDING

Binding cushion edges or frills adds a smart finish for relatively little extra cost. Sometimes the binding fabric can be chosen to contrast with the main fabric, but most usually it is selected to tone with the whole, or to emphasise a colour already in the main fabric. For example, a blue and white print would usually be edged with a blue binding, not a white one.

I use 1.5 cm (⅝ in) as an average size, but each binding will depend on the size and type of cushion. Generally, small cushions work best with a narrow binding and larger cushions, a wider one. If in doubt, choose a narrower binding.

BORDERS

Borders in a contrast colour or texture set around the edge of a cushion or inset into the cushion front give a tailored finish and define the cushion shape.

Draw your cushion, or pin pieces of fabric to the pad, and decide how many and how deep to make each border. Cut fabric pieces for the whole cushion to make up a template, adding 1.5 cm (⅝ in) seam allowance to each cut edge. The centre of the cushion will be cut as a whole panel and the borders stitched along each side before mitring the corner. So if your cushion is to be 50 cm (20 in) square with an outer border of 3 cm (1¼ in) and an inner border set 3 cm (1¼ in) in you will need to cut a total of 13 pieces for the cushion front.

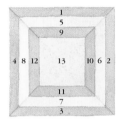

1. Join sides 9/10/11/12 to the centre piece (13) one at a time, stopping and securing stitched 1.5 cm (⅝ in) for each side of each corner.

2. Join 5/6/7/8 to the 9/10/11/12 piece, stitching to the end of each piece. Repeat with sides 1/2/3/4. Press all seams flat.

3. Pin across each corner to mitre, and adjust pins as necessary so that the cushion and each corner sits absolutely flat on to the worktable. Stitch along the pin line and press.

4. Continue to make up following the instructions for plain, piped or bordered cushions.

Cut sizes including seam allowances:

Sides 1/2/3/4	53 × 6 cm (21 × 2¼ in)
Sides 5/6/7/8	47 × 6 cm (18½ × 2¼ in)
Sides 9/10/11/12	41 × 6 cm (16 × 2¼ in)
Centre 13	35 × 35 cm (13¾ × 13¾ in)

INSERTING A ZIP

All cushions need to be made up with a zip fastener inserted into the back seam, so that the cover can be removed for cleaning. Below, we show two methods for inserting a zip. The first method is probably the most simple and straightforward, and the one used throughout the book. The second method is used when inserting a zip into a piped seam and is ideal when you want the zip to be invisible, such as on a cushion which is seen from all sides.

Method 1

1. Pin one side of the zip to the opening, 2 mm (⅛ in) away from the teeth. Machine top stitch this half of the zip in place.

2. Machine the other side of the opening to the zip forming a flap to encase the teeth. The zip itself should not be visible on completion.

Method 2

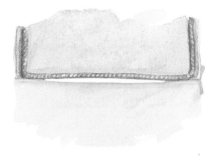

1. Apply the piping to the front of the fabric. Join the front and back pieces together, allowing a gap for the zip.

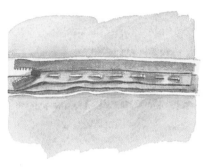

2. Pin one side of the zip against the piping line on the front of the cushion from the wrong side. Machine stitch tightly in place.

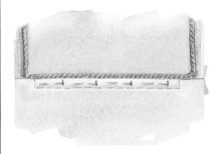

3. Open out the cushion seam and carefully pin the other side of the zip in position, ensuring that the fabric butts up to the piping without gaping. Machine stitch in place, carefully stitching across the ends of the zip to prevent the head becoming lost.

MEASURING FOR CUSHIONS

Before you make up shaped or seat cushions, it will be necessary to make a simple template from calico or paper to help you ensure the cushion fits into the seat snugly and correctly.

SOFAS AND ARMCHAIRS

When making new box seat and back cushion covers for sofas and armchairs, you should always take your measurements from the actual upholstered furniture rather than either the old cushions or the old covers. Covers may well have shrunk in the wash, and pads will

become misshapen with use. As the cushions of sofas and chairs will need to be laundered, either choose pre-shrunk fabrics or allow 3–5 per cent for the first wash shrinkage.

To make a template of the arm curve, take a square of calico or cotton fabric and pin to the side of the chair or sofa. Snip along the arm to the back, until the fabric lies flat against both the arm and the chair back. Cut around the arm of the chair so that the cushion cover will fit snugly.

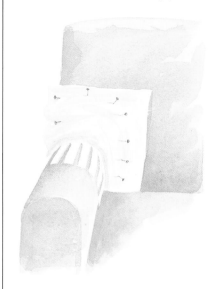

If you prefer the look of Turkish-style cushion covers, make boxed sections for the back and Turkish corners on the front only. Make fabric templates by pinning the top and bottom together over the pads to find a neat piping line along the centre of the gusset depth and gather the corners tightly.

WINDOW SEATS AND SETTLES

Window seat cushions, especially those which will be used as seating, need to fit quite tightly into the seat space to prevent them from falling forwards every time someone gets up to walk away. To prevent this happening, you can employ a number of measures. Popper tabs are one solution: fit one half of a popper tab strip to the back of the cushion cover and staple the other half to the window seat. Another option is to attach touch and close tape. Alternatively, you could stitch on ties which reach right under the seat itself.

The most obvious measurements for your pad and cover are those from side to side and front to back. Even with a seemingly symmetrical seat, always check the back, front, left and right sides and the vertical front to back, as you will be surprised how very few seats are true and 'square'.

If your window seat is set into an angled recess, make sure that you measure an exact rectangle

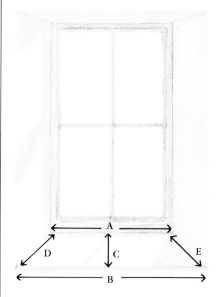

A: back
B: front
C: front to back
D: left side
E: right side

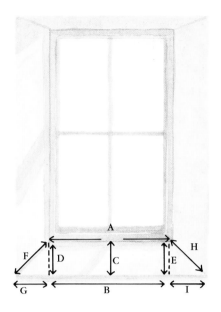

A: back
B: front
C: front to back
D: front to back
E: front to back
F: left side
G: left side to right angle
H: right side
I: right side to right angle

for the centre of the seat, and make a template of each side. It is rare to find a seat with equal sides, and a paper template is the only way to ensure a snug fit.

If you choose to make a firm pad, the cushion will not be reversible, so you might consider using a heavy twill platform lining or plain canvas on the underside (especially if you have chosen an expensive or extravagant fabric for the top).

Should you need to make the pad reversible, and the sides are almost, but not quite even, then use a feather pad which will be much more malleable and adaptable than a piece of rubberised hair or foam. This can then be moulded into shape.

SQUAB CUSHIONS

Squab cushions add a decorative, welcoming touch to a chair seat, but their primary function is to make a hard chair seat more comfortable. For this reason, the pads must be deep enough to be soft, but not so soft that the wood or metal seat still feels hard through the cushion. The pad must also fit well enough so as not to move around when you are sitting on it. Foam or rubberised hair with a wadding wrap are the best pad solutions for this type of seat cushion.

You will need to cut a template from the actual chair seat to use as an accurate pattern for the seat shapes. Either paper, or tightly woven cotton are suitable, but for this purpose, I prefer newspaper, which is soft enough to fold and tear easily to fit around difficult leg and arm interruptions. A thick pencil is useful to mark the edges

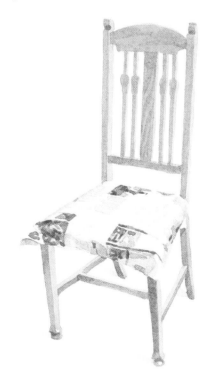

of the seat on to the paper, and sticky tape will help hold the folds and tears into place. I then transfer this pattern to heavier brown paper from which I cut the fabric and pad patterns.

If you are in any doubt – for instance, if the chair seat is shaped on all sides and also within the seat itself – cut a pattern from calico or other strong fabric and lie this on the seat to check the shape, before cutting your main fabric.

Tape paper to the back, front and sides of the chair seat. Bend the paper along the shaped seat and confirm the line with a thick pencil. Tear and fold the paper around the arms and legs to give you a really accurate shape. Remember, you can always stick a bit back on if you over-cut. The important thing is to fit the paper surely enough to gain an accurate template from which to cut your final pattern.

FILLINGS

Traditionally, straw or horsehair was stitched tightly into seat pads covered with cotton covers, but these are too hard for today's more comfortable lifestyle and so a variety of standard cushion fillings to suit varying needs has been adapted and is readily available. Feather and down mixes make comfortable, squashy pads; foam pads are firm but not too comfortable, while a compromise might be a foam pad covered with fibre or feather wrap for neatness and comfort.

SOFT FILLINGS

Duck or goose down makes the most luxurious and longest lasting cushion filling, but is also very expensive. The high cost of 100 per cent down fillings is prohibitive, so a feather/down mix is often preferred. The most common option is down and feathers in a 40:60 per cent proportion, but this gives a mediocre filling which will need plumping up regularly. Try to find at least a 60 per cent down:40 per cent feather filling for a sofa seat cushion which will hold its shape well and plump up satisfactorily. Down will stay fluffy for years, while feathers will eventually uncurl, flatten and need to be replaced. Always overstuff the cushions initially to allow for the inevitable sinking which will occur once the cushions are in regular use.

Recently there has been some welcome development with both wool and cotton fillings. Wool cushions are extremely comfortable and are especially useful as narrow pads over stiff, upholstered seats, especially on antique show-wood sofas and Victorian chesterfields.

Cotton pads are soft but firm rather than squashy. Cotton fibres enclosed in canvas covers are stitched through at regular intervals to hold the pad in shape. Particularly used for metal framed rocking chairs, campaign chairs and sofas, these seat pads are strong enough to sit over the metal framework but soft enough for comfort.

FIRM FILLINGS

Some people dislike the crumpled look which a soft filling gives, so a firm cushion filling is needed. The most usual will be a piece of foam with a thick polyester wadding wrap to soften the seat. Foam cushions are available in a several price bands, according to the quality and construction of the cushion. The best and most comfortable have been carefully constructed from several layers of foam in varying weights with a hard centre core and gradually softer layers. These cushions still have the firm look but are very comfortable to sit on. The least expensive, single foam cushions are either so hard that you sit rather stiffly 'on' them or so soft that they quickly flatten.

Horsehair pads sit well on traditional formal chairs, settles and some window casement seats, and are a preferable alternative to foam slabs. Horsehair is rather expensive and time consuming to make up, so rubberised coconut fibre pads make a suitable and adequate substitute. These are available from upholstery suppliers in large pads or cut to size. The pad might be prickly so it should be covered with cotton wadding or interlining and then a cover of calico stitched tightly over the top.

MIXED FILLINGS

A recent development has been the creation of mixed fillings for cushion and seat pads, and a good quality foam cushion interior with a quilted feather wrap is now available. Although only specialist furniture makers currently supply these, they do go some way to solving the problem between the look of the seat cushion, the comfort and maintenance. As long as the best quality foam is used, cushions made with these pads will look smart and stay comfortable for many years.

Another solution which is much less expensive and more widely available is a filling made with a mixture of fibre and feathers, or fibre only. But these are not long term solutions, as the fibre will eventually matt together and the edges which have been sat on regularly will become irretrievably misshapen.

Many people compromise by combining some sort of foam cushion on the seat and feather/down back cushions, which are more comfortable to sink into.

MAKING A SIMPLE PAD

Use this for squab or window seat cushions. Cut a piece of foam or rubberised hair to the template. Cut cotton wadding or interlining to fit all around the pad.

1. Wrap the pad with the wadding or interlining, leaving enough at each edge to fold up over the sides, starting and finishing at the back to keep the front seam-free. Fold the sides and back to one edge, trim away excess so that the pad is now enclosed. Stitch interlining together or cover the wadding with calico. Pull the top and bottom together at the back and stitch the raw edges together.

2. Cover this pad with lining in the same way, making a gusset at either end. Hand stitch all around three sides to enclose the pad.

SCATTER CUSHIONS

Scatter cushions need to be soft and comfortable, to be able to mould around the body easily. The very best filling is a mix of down and feather, but economy dictates that most cushions will have a large percentage of feathers. Down, being soft and fluffy, will respond to being plumped up for as many years as you wish – the tiny fibres fill with air immediately. If there is a chance of finding an eiderdown from a parent or grandparent which may be externally damaged, use the filling for your best cushions.

Basic feather fillings are curled poultry feathers which have been cured and wrapped in a feather-proof ticking case. In time, the feathers will uncurl and once flat have little means of trapping air. It is a false economy to re-stuff an old cushion – it will just become heavy and flatten even more quickly. Replace the pad. If you are allergic to feathers then a fibre filling is a reasonable alternative. Fibre will never quite give the fullness of a feather pad and may well become misshapen in a relatively short period of time.

Avoid kapok or foam chip fillings as these are always lumpy.

Many sizes and shapes of pad are readily available from large department stores and any unusual or over-sized pads may be ordered through a soft furnishings specialist or interior decorator. Choose your pads carefully. If you want to make a cushion to fit into the small of the back, test an old one to find the size which is most comfortable once it has been flattened. Always scale the cushion size to the sofa size. Some modern sofas are very deep, and normal 43 cm (17 in) cushions will look completely lost.

It is fun to use very large cushions or very small cushions for decoration. Experiment with groupings and sizes. Perhaps a pile of three or four large cushions on the floor or a small 30 cm (12 in) cushion sitting at the back of a formal side chair.

Scatter cushions are accessories and although used for comfort at times, for the most part of the day, the function is purely decorative. It doesn't much matter which cushion is used where once a room is full of people, but for first impressions each cushion should be in its place.

Before you can choose the fabrics, the colours and the pad sizes, you will need to have chosen the room style. You might prefer a formal setting, with structured, tailored cushions, or you might wish to introduce a contrast by adding frills and cords. In either case, the size for pad and finish will be very important as each cushion will be a statement, and need to be chosen with the scale of the room and furniture in mind. Use a pillow or other cushions and offcuts of fabric to help you plan.

If you have chosen an informal room, then a mix of pad sizes will be needed: large and small squares and rectangles with perhaps bolsters and round box cushions. Again, planning is the reason for success. The rule of thumb is to buy a pad size 2.5 cm (1 in) larger than the cover size.

PREPARATION

Preparation is the key to successful sewing. Look at various factors before you begin: where you are going to work, what you plan to work on and the fabric you plan to use. Allow enough material to match any design, and work out how best to place templates to avoid unnecessary waste.

Plan out the size and positions for your cushions first for maximum impact and ultimate comfort.

Here are some basic guidelines to bear in mind before you begin sewing.

CUSHION SIZES

As you spend time choosing the shapes and fabrics for your sofa and chairs cushions, so the sizes and mix of sizes is important. Deep and fixed back sofas will need large cushions full enough to support yet soft enough for comfort, and small sofas will need cushions which mould easily.

Cushions should always be chosen in proportion to the sofa or chair and arranged for effect, yet still be easily rearranged to accommodate people sitting. A mixture of cushion sizes, some of which can be placed into the small of the back and moved to support the head and/or arms is important.

THE WORKTABLE

Although it is not essential for sewing small items, like cushions, it is better if you can stake your claim on one room which can be put aside for your use.

A dining room or guest bedroom can be made into a temporary workroom with little effort. A worktable which is about 2.5 × 1.2 m (8 × 4 ft) will make sewing so much easier. You can buy a sheet of board in this size, and if you cover your dining table with thick felt, the board can be rested on top.

Alternatively, make some sturdy legs which can be bracketed on to the underside of the board. This quickly-made table can then be fitted temporarily over a guest bed. The space below can be used to store all your fabrics and the top will be wide enough for you to work. Pure luxury compared to the kitchen table!

The height of the worktable should be whatever is comfortable for you; I use a table that is 95 cm (38 in) high.

Cover the top with heavy interlining and then a layer of lining. Staple these to the underside; pulling the fabrics taut as you go. You will now have a soft surface which is ideal for pinning and pressing.

CUTTING OUT

Before you begin to cut the fabric, check it thoroughly for flaws. Try to cut away simple line flaws or incorporate them into seams or hems. If the fabric is badly flawed, return it to the retailer.

Measure out each piece carefully and mark with pins to make sure that you have the correct amount of fabric, and always double check your measurements before cutting.

Fabric should ideally be cut along the grain and to pattern, but sometimes the printing method allows the pattern to move off grain. Do not be tempted to follow the pattern and cut off the grain, as the finished cushions could look odd.

PATTERN MATCHING

1. Place one of the cuts of fabric right side up on to the worktable with the selvedge facing you. Place the next cut over the first, right side down. Fold over the selvedge showing approximately 5 mm (¼ in) of the pattern and press lightly.

2. Match the pattern to the piece underneath, and pin through the fold line along the whole length. You may need to ease one of the sides at times – using more pins will help. Go back and place cross pins between each pin. Machine or hand stitch along the fold line, removing the straight pins and stitching over the cross pins.

3. Press the seam from the wrong side and then again from the front. Use a very hot iron and press quickly. Turn over again to the back and press under the seam to remove the pressed ridges. If the background fabric is dark or you are using a woven fabric, snip into the selvedges at approximately 5 cm (2 in) intervals. If the background fabric is light, trim the selvedges back to 1.5 cm (⅝ in), removing any writing printed on the edges.

PLACING THE PATTERN

If you have made a paper template of the chair seat or window seat, transfer this to calico or scrap fabric and add 2 cm (¾ in) all round for seams. If the cushions are square or rectangular, measure carefully and note the longest and widest measurements. Add 2 cm (¾ in) all round for seam allowances. Measure gussets, frills, piping and note the sizes needed, adding seam allowances.

Plan these pieces (top, bottom, gusset, piping, etc) on the worktable to see how they fit into the fabric width. If you are making several cushions which go together, they must be planned thoughtfully to obtain maximum benefit from the fabric.

If the fabric has a dominant pattern, the pieces will need to be planned so that the cushions are cut together to prevent wastage of fabric. If possible, make the cushion covers reversible.

On seat and back cushions, patterns should always read from front to back. The gusset should be placed so that the pattern follows through and matches exactly. Piping may be cut on the cross or on the straight. If the cushion has straight sides, then the choice is yours; if there are any curves or curved corners, cut on the cross so that the piping can be bent and still lie flat.

As a general rule, allow 1 metre (1 yard) of fabric for each seat. So allow approximately 2 m (2¼ yd) for a two-seat sofa.

Also allow for pattern repeats. Small geometric patterns and all-over designs need approximately 10 per cent extra fabric; large prints may need almost double the amount a plain fabric will take. Fabric bindings need to be of similar weight to the main fabric, or instead try wide ribbon, linen tape or upholstery webbing.

BASIC CUSHION

Basic scatter cushions provide decoration and comfort, but need not be at all complicated to make. A simple basic cushion can add an instant splash of colour, and only takes minutes to make.

MAKING UP

Cut out two pieces of fabric, one for the front and one for the back, placing any pattern to its best advantage and allowing 1.5 cm (⅝ in) seam allowance all round.

1. Place the front and back pieces together, right sides facing. Snip or make notches through both layers, randomly on each side.

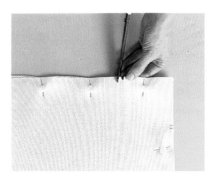

2. Pin the two pieces together along the bottom edge and stitch for 4 cm (1½ in) from each side. Put in the zip following instructions on page 11.

Although extremely simple to make, a group of scatter cushions can add a finishing flourish to any room. Instead of piped edges, these cushions have been trimmed with thick cord.

3. Open the zip about halfway and pin the other three cushion sides together, taking care to match the notches. Trim across each corner.

4. As far as possible, press the seams flat. Turn the cushion right side out and press the seam line along each side lightly.

Finishing Touches

● Stitch cord all around with small stitches, weaving into the cord and through the edge of the cushion cover so that stitches are invisible. Knot each corner and stitch in place.

● Inset fan edging braid by stitching it to the front piece before the zip is inserted.

● Cut and twisted fringes, tassels and braids can be stitched to two or four sides with small stitches holding each edge in place.

● Make a rolled edge by inserting a twist of polyester wadding or soft interlining against the outer edge once the cushion cover has been turned to the front. Stitch the roll in place using a decorative hand stitch. Alternatively, machine stitch and cover the line with cord.

Bright silks in varying tones and hues were made into basic scatter cushions (right) for a quick, but effective, splash of colour on this formal striped sofa.

APPLIED TRIMMINGS

A veritable host of trimmings is now available for the enthusiastic soft furnishings maker. However, applied trimmings should always be chosen carefully so that they

Using textures and colours similar in tone gives a very sophisticated finish. Silks in off-white and palest cream complement the hand woven silk damask in pure white. Cords in two sizes, a giroline braid and elaborate fringe in white, off-white and gold transform the simplest unpiped cushions into luxurious accessories.

add to the fabrics used and the cushion shapes made, becoming part of the whole, rather than a strong factor demanding attention. So often, understated single colours and colour mixes will best bring out the character of the fabrics but the trimming itself can be as elaborate as you like.

Only three colour tones – off-white, pure white and palest cream – have been used here, but the textures of the fabrics embrace matt to high sheen. Plain weave silks with a slight sheen, hand printed gold lustre over a checked weave with hand woven damask complement the simple drapes made from an interesting combination of fine linen over inexpensive jute scrim.

1. A narrow cord stitched all around is just enough to finish the cushion edge, while giroline braid has been hand stitched on both sides to hold it in place.
2. Giroline bends easily to make a circle, but needs to be stitched around both outer and inner circumferences. The most exquisite fringe decorates the sides.
3. Decorative detail here is added with the giroline stitched straight along the side edges and narrow cord on the other two sides parallel to the giroline.
4. Narrow flanged cord stitched between the off-white and pale cream silks echoes the wider cord which has been stitched around the outside of the cushion and knotted at each corner.

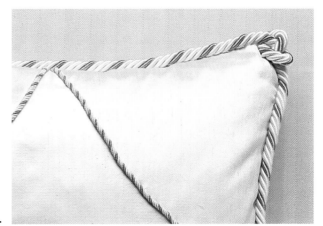

1

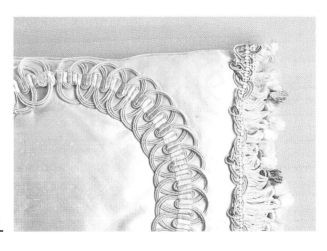

2

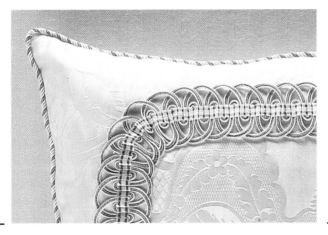

3

4

SCATTER CUSHIONS

Keeping to one principal colour and one neutral colour, mix stripes with checks, add plain woven tapes, scalloped edges and piping cords for a fun collection of scatter cushions.

If your time is limited or your patience with making furnishings is in short supply, then stick to the most basic piped and unpiped scatter cushions, playing with colours, patterns, tones, hues, textures and trimmings, to add vital accents to your scheme and to accessorise your chairs, sofas and beds. If, on the other hand, making has become a passion and collecting pieces of fabric your forte, then you can spend many happy hours mixing and matching fabrics to create endless patterns, shapes and designs within each cushion.

By keeping the same colour scheme, but using various patterns, weaves and textures, you can produce a very sophisticated effect. But if you prefer an abundance of country floral prints or a combination of contrasting plain colours, then the addition of tapes, cords, braids or borders in one colour will serve to hold the other colours and patterns together and to identify the form of each cushion so preventing a chaotic mess.

PIPED SCATTER CUSHION

MAKING UP

1. Cut the cushion front and back, placing any pattern to its best advantage, and adding 1.5 cm (⁵⁄₈ in) all round for seams. Cut a strip the width of the cushion × 7 cm (2¾ in) and match it to the bottom 7 cm (2¾ in) of the back piece. Make up piping to go all round.

2. Place the two pieces on to the worktable, right sides together and snip or notch randomly all around.

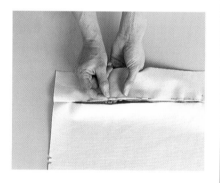

3. Press the bottom edge of the back piece under by 5 cm (2 in) and trim back to 2 cm (¾ in). Pin the extra strip along the fold line. Stitch together along the fold from each side, continuing along the fold lines.

4. Insert the zip following the instructions on page 11. Open the zip to roughly halfway.

5. Pin the piping to the front piece, starting from the bottom centre, snipping and folding hard into the corners. Pin and join following the instructions on page 10. Stitch on.

6. With right sides together, pin the front to the back, working from the front side, matching notches or snips. Sew inside the piping stitching line and very close to the piping cord.

7. Turn right side out. If any of the piping stitching is showing or the piping looks uneven, stitch around again. Trim the corners and stitch across them to secure. Finish the seams and turn out. Press gently along the piping lines and pull each corner square. Fill with the cushion pad, plumping it well to ensure that the corners have enough padding.

DECORATIVE OPTIONS

1. Stitch decorative braids to your cushion front before adding the piping. Stitch two strips of 5 mm (¼ in) tape first and then two strips of 3 mm (⅛ in) tape over the top.

2. Scalloped borders in matching or contrasting fabric need to be made up and stitched to the piped cushion front before the front and back pieces are stitched together.

3. An easier way to make a scalloped border is to over-cut the cushion fronts and backs, cutting the shaped edge around the front piece only. Fine piping is a little difficult to add but need not be a problem if pinned carefully and snipped often so that it lies flat. Pin the front to the back and stitch from the front close to the piping. Snip away all excess fabric, turn out, press, pin and satin stitch together.

4. The cushion front can either be joined in three panels or can be made to appear as three sections by stitching the centre piece over the cushion front. Use braids or tapes to cover the joins, stitching close to each side. Pipe the cushion front and make up in the usual way.

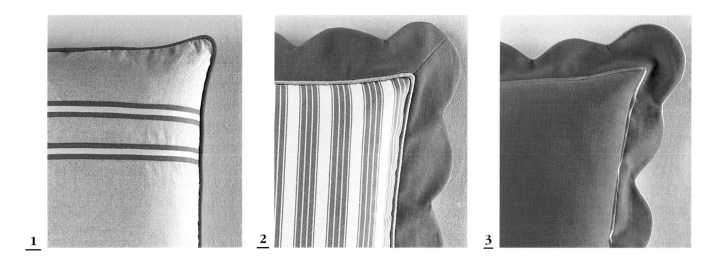

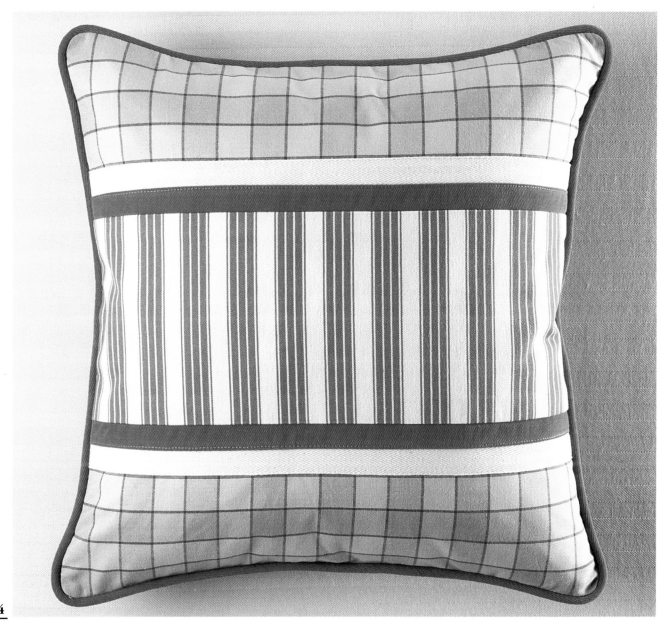

FRILLED CUSHIONS

Frilled edges are usually added to give a feminine touch, especially when used alongside floral fabrics, lace trimmings and bedroom furnishings. Frilled edges may be as a short, tight ruche or cut to be long and floppy, so adding weight to the sides which can improve the way a cushion sits on the arm of a chair or sofa, for instance.

Frills can be used with any fabric: do not feel restricted to florals.

MAKING UP

Cut pieces for the back and front, placing any pattern to its best advantage and adding 1.5 cm (⅝ in) all round for seams. Cut a strip of fabric the width of the cushion × 7 cm (2¾ in) and match to the bottom 7 cm (2¾ in) of the back. Make up piping to go all round. Cut strips for frills, allowing at least double fullness. For a simple frill allow twice the depth of the finished frill, plus seam allowance.

1. Press the bottom edge of the back piece under 5 cm (2 in) and trim to 2 cm (¾ in). Pin the extra strip to this piece, right sides together, along the fold line. Stitch together 4 cm (1½ in) from each side, along the fold line.

2. Insert the zip following the instructions on page 11. Open the zip to about halfway.

3. Pin piping to the front piece, starting at the centre bottom, snipping and folding firmly into each corner. Pin and join following the instructions on page 10.

4. Make up the frills, joining the strips together along the short sides. Press the seams flat, fold in half lengthways wrong sides together and stitch a gathering thread 1.3 cm (½ in) from the raw edges. Divide the frill length by eight and mark with coloured tacks. Also mark halfway along each side of the cushion front in the same way. Gather the frill slightly. Using the tacks as markers, pin the frill to the cushion front, matching the tacks to each corner and to each side.

5. With the frill pinned at the coloured tacks, pull up the gathers evenly between these points. Pin along the piping line and across the piping. Stitch as close to the piping cord as possible, leaving the pins across the piping in place while stitching.

6. Remove the pins, turn the cushion over and check that the piping stitching line is not visible. If it is, re-stitch inside the previous line to ensure you have a really neat finish.

7. Pin the back of the cushion to the front, matching corners and notches. Stitch close to the piping line as before. Cut across the corners and stitch to secure. Turn right side out, pull corners square, press and fill with the pad.

I like to add frills to otherwise quite strong or 'masculine' fabrics, such as this strong navy and white stripe, rather than to make an overtly frilly cushion. The frill introduces a gentleness and softness to a formal situation.

MAKING BACKED AND BOUND FRILLS

For a frill which shows 8 cm (3¼ in) including a 1.5 cm (⅝ in) binding when finished, cut the front strips 9.5 cm (3¾ in) wide and the back strips 12.5 cm (4¾ in) wide.

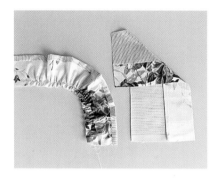

Join the short sides to make two lengths. Stitch the lengths together, with a 1.4 cm (⅝ in) seam allowance. This seam allowance must be stitched accurately. Stitch the short ends together to make a loop. Press the fabrics from the right side, pressing towards the binding fabric. Fold under so that 1.5 cm (⅝ in) of binding remains visible on the front. Pin all round. Stitch a gathering thread all around, 1.5 cm (⅝ in) from the raw edges.

BOUND FRILLS

For a frill which shows 8 cm (3¼ in) of the same fabric on both front and back, finished with 1.5 cm (⅝ in) binding, cut two strips 9.5 cm (3¾ in) wide and one binding strip 5.5 cm (2⅛ in) wide.

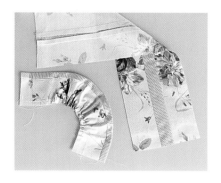

Join the short sides to make two lengths; press the seams flat. Stitch one edge of the binding to the front of the frill 1.4 cm (⅝ in) from the raw edges. Stitch the other side of the binding to the back frill, 1.4 cm (⅝ in) from the edges. Stitch the short ends together to make a loop, trimming the fabric as necessary. Press the seams towards the binding. Fold in half so that the binding is exactly equal all along and the seams fit right into the fold line. Run a gathering thread all around, 1.5 cm (⅝ in) from the raw edges.

Frills can be made up in double or triple layers, and gathered very fully. Edges can be stitched under or finished with ribbons or, as on these unlined frills, a lovely picot-edged lace.

BUTTERFLY FRILLED CUSHION

A frilled edge may be added to the face of a cushion rather than stitched between the front and back pieces. The frill is piped or bound along both sides and needs to be made up first and stitched in position so that the frill lies on to the front of the cushion rather than falling away at the sides. This type of frill is called a 'butterfly' frill because as it is stitched, the inner edge lifts up.

MAKING UP

Cut out two pieces of fabric for the front and back, placing any pattern to its best advantage. Cut an extra strip the width of the cushion × 5 cm (2 in) and match to the bottom of the back piece. Cut two strips for the frill, allowing at least double fullness (measure around the outside of the pieces). For a 9 cm (3½ in) frill, cut pieces 12 cm (4¾ in) wide. Cut enough piping or binding for both sides of the frill, each 3 cm (1¼ in) wide.

1. Join the front and back strips for the frill as two lengths. If using piping, make up and pin to both long sides of one of the frill pieces, 1.5 cm (⅝ in) in from the raw edges. Stitch in place. If using binding, press in half lengthways and stitch as for piping, 5 mm (¼ in) from the folded edge.

2. Pin the other frill piece over and stitch close to the piping or binding stitching line.

3. Trim the seams to 1 cm (³⁄₈ in). Turn right side out and press along the two edges.

4. Stitch the two short ends together carefully, lining up the piping and seams. Stitch a gathering thread 2.5–3cm (1–1¹⁄₄ in) from one edge.

5. Divide the length of the frill by eight and mark with coloured tacks. Sew a marking tack halfway along each side of the cushion front. Pin the frill to the cushion front with the gathering line 6 cm (2¹⁄₄ in) in from the edge. Match the tacks on the frill to the corners and the tacks along the sides.

6. Stitch into place with a 2 × 2 zig zag stitch. Remove all the gathering threads.

The opulent touch of a butterfly frill (above) gives an added flourish to an otherwise fairly simple patterned fabric. When combined with a striped chair seat cushion, the overall effect is classical yet cosy.

7. Press under 5 cm (2 in) at the bottom edge of the back piece and trim back to 2 cm (³⁄₄ in). Pin the extra piece to the back, along the fold line. Stitch along the fold line for 4 cm (1¹⁄₂ in) from each side. Stitch the zip into the opening following instructions on page 11 and open halfway.

8. Pin the cushion back to the cushion front, avoiding the frill. Stitch all around and neaten the seam. Turn right side out and fill.

The mid-blue in the rich floral pattern is echoed in the smart ticking stripe of the double frill. The same bold stripe has been used to make the piping, to give a neat and detailed finish.

IDEAS FOR FRILLS

Frills give the opportunity to introduce other elements to the design: for example, another fabric, a contrasting piping or a toning binding.

1. Mixing fabrics is one of the challenges and joys of making your own soft furnishings – always keep your offcuts – colour coded for easy reference; you never know when they might come in useful. This fine shirt stripe, which was trimmed from the lining of some former curtains, makes the perfect backing for this floral design.

Double frills are pretty and very extravagant with fabric but take little extra time to make. The outer frill should be made to finish approximately 1.5 cm (⅝ in) wider than the inner one. Cut and stitch lengths separately, fold and press lengthways then pin together using one gathering thread through both frills. Make up as one.

2. It is fun to use another fabric to pipe the cushion and to bind the frills. Stripes add a little formality and smartness to pretty floral motifs. I like this two-toned stripe because it is so subtle. The piping could have been cut on the cross or on the straight; I rather like the combination here.

One of the keys to making successful furnishings is a clever combination of fabrics, which will keep a visitor wondering why a room looks so inviting without being able to pinpoint the reason.

3. A subtle cotton print in the same tones as the buttermilk stripe of the main fabric is just enough to bind the frill and pipe the cushion, adding a professional finish which is neither demanding nor boring. Some of the best chintzes are those that have two patterns designed and printed to complement each other – in this case a beautifully coloured bouquet of Gallica roses over a delicately printed background.

4. If a plain colour is preferred to finish a cushion it should not be overbearing. Always choose to tone with the other colours rather than attempting an exact match. Take the colour from the mid to lighter tonal range rather than the deepest end of the scale. The green chosen is yellow-olive to tone with the buttermilk ground – a harder or deeper green would have killed the wonderful colouring of the roses, but a lighter or softer green would have been fine. The frills were placed and cut to include as much of the green leaves as possible. To prevent the possibility of overpowering further, the piping uses very small cord and the double frills are the same depth, so that the outer frill just peeps through as the frills are separated.

5. Instead of using another fabric, detail can be added by using ready made trimmings: cords, fringes, braids, ribbons, buttons, lace and tassels can all be added to frilled cushions. Some people find piping very difficult to master and one way to overcome this is to stitch a cord to the finished cushion in the place of piping. Or should your piping be less perfect than you had hoped, stitch a cord or fringe over the top to disguise the embarrassment. Trimmings should almost always pick up the tones and colourings that are already present in the main fabric. I selected a cord twisted with apricot, pink and cream to pick up the lovely petals, but a soft buttery mix or pale olive tones could have been used equally as effectively.

6. Compare this cushion to number 4, to see the astonishingly different effect that can be created when other pieces of the pattern are used to make the frills and different ends of the colour spectrum are picked up from the same design.

This cushion is much lighter in feel, with almost none of the stronger colours being present in the frills, and a plain binding which tones with the very palest apricot in the petals. A slightly stronger peach tone has been used for the piping to add more substance to the whole. The choice of finish is not just personal but also bears in mind the situation in which each cushion will be placed. Both cushions would look wonderful placed on a buttermilk, peach or apricot chair, but one would look better in a room where other furnishings are covered with predominantly light colours and one where other furnishings are in deeper tones.

1

2

3

4

5

6

BORDERED
CUSHIONS

**Sometimes one single cushion is all
that is needed to add both necessary
comfort and a vital splash of colour to
a simply furnished room.**

Bordered cushions can be made in one of two ways: by stitching an inner line on an unpiped cushion which will contain the pad, or by folding extra fabric under on both front and back, along all four sides and stitching to make flaps. The latter are known as Oxford cushions and the former as false Oxford cushions, being much easier to make and taking considerably less fabric.

In both methods the bordered width must be added to the pad measurement before planning and cutting.

Use bordered cushions with piped and unpiped cushions to add a change of scale, and use with frilled and piped cushions to add some formality. The added border helps the cushion to stay in position, either on the arm of a chair or sofa or on a chair seat. They are also ideal for outside use on garden chairs or made over-sized as floor cushions.

FALSE OXFORD

Add the required border width to the pad width and allow 1.5 cm (⅝ in) all round for seams. Cut the front piece to these measurements, placing any pattern to its best advantage. Cut two pieces for the back, the same width as the front, but one piece 12 cm (4¾ in) deep and the other 10 cm (4 in) shorter than the front piece.

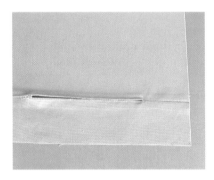

1. Press 2 cm (¾ in) under along the lower edge of the larger back piece. Pin the 12 cm (4¾ in) strip to it, along the fold line and stitch 12 cm (4¾ in) in from either side. Insert the zip, as explained on page 11 and open halfway.

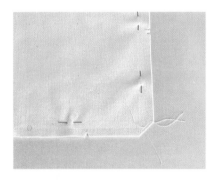

2. Pin the front and back pieces, right sides together. Stitch all round. Trim across the corners and sew over again to strengthen.

3. Neaten the seams and turn right side out. Press along all the sides and pin all around to prevent any slipping.

4. Measure the width of the border carefully from each side and mark a line with light pencil or vanishing pen. Pin across the line at approximately 4 cm (1½ in) intervals. Satin stitch closely along this line to define the border.

There are many ways to finish a border: try sewing several rows of satin stitch in the same colour or mixed colours to contrast or pick out the cushion fabric. Or stitch braid over the top with a straight stitching line. Satin stitch always takes more thread than you might expect, so make sure that the bobbin is full before each row.

A true Oxford cushion (above) – notice the two separate flaps – will sit comfortably into the back of almost any upholstered chair.

QUILTING

Quilting bordered cushions does take a little longer but the result is well worth any extra effort. Quilting either the front only or both front and back can also change the appearance of the cushion completely.

MAKING UP

1. Cut the main pieces of fabric just slightly larger than the finished cushion to allow the fabric to puff up a little – 5 per cent should be enough. Cut two layers of 50 g or 100 g (2 oz or 4 oz) polyester wadding and one piece of calico or fine cotton to the same size. Place the calico flat on to the worktable with the wadding and then place the main fabric on top.

2. Pin the layers together all around the sides. Pin across the centre from top to bottom and from left to right, tack to secure using double thread. Also tack around the outside. I find that a back stitch every so often really helps to hold the fabrics together.

3. Mark out your chosen design, bearing in mind the pad size and where the border and the seam allowances will be. Pencil and tack the lines carefully for a complex design. If you have chosen a simple pattern, mark it with a light pencil and pins. Tacking can help, but I prefer to use a softly marked line and pins, as it can be difficult to remove the tacking threads if they become caught up with the machine stitches.

4. Once the pieces have been quilted and you are satisfied with the effect, make up the cushion following the instructions on page 34.

I like to use quilting where the main fabric might be liable to crease, and in rooms full of textures and textiles, especially studies, libraries and family rooms (below). Quilting adds a richness and extra dimension to patterned fabrics, which renders the additional time spent more than worthwhile.

I prefer to quilt with large squares but small squares, diamonds, hexagons, circles, outline or vermicelli quilting, single or double rows are all possible alternatives.

PIPED BORDERS

Separate borders piped to the main cushion allow contrasts in colour and pattern, but are very much more difficult to make accurately; attempt these only if you are experienced. The white on white makes an extremely elegant cushion, the yellow and green cushions could be used in the most classical and formal of rooms.

DESIGN AND MAKE CUSHIONS

MAKING UP

Cut the front piece to the pad size, allowing 1.5 cm (⅝ in) for seams. Cut the back to the pad size plus the border width and the seam allowance, allowing an extra 4 cm (1½ in) for the zip opening. Cut away 11 cm (4¼ in) from the bottom. Stitch together again, 12 cm (4¾ in) in from each side and insert the zip following the instructions on page 11. Pipe the cushion front.

1. Cut four strips of fabric the width of the finished border plus 3 cm (1¼ in) for seams and the length of each side, plus two border widths. Pin one border strip to the bottom of the cushion front and one to the side, starting at the centre. Mark the first corner, unpin the strip and fold to make a right angle. Stitch together along this fold line.

2. Pin the border once again on to the cushion front, and join to the two corners. Mark carefully, repeating the folding and stitching instructions.

3. Repeat with the final corner. Stitch each side in turn, unpicking the stitching on each mitre 1.5 cm (⅝ in) so that the corner lies flat. Stitch as closely to the piping as possible, secure the stitching at each corner and start with the needle position exactly along the mitre line.

4. Stitch the back to the front, secure the corners and turn right sides out. Pin the front and back pieces together and stitch along the piping line through all layers.

If you enjoy whitework, cross stitching or any other stitchwork use your skills to embellish the bordered edges.

BORDER OPTIONS

1. A padded rolled border gives a plump and sumptuous finish to the cushion, yet is quite straight-forward to make. To add a padded roll, make up the cushion as the following instructions. Add a border to the front and back cushion pieces. Stitch together, then make a polyester wadding or interlining roll (sometimes you can buy ready made foam rolls) and push into the border. Pin along the border edge and machine or hand stitch to hold in place.

2. Adding double borders to the basic cushion is a great achievement for an extremely smart and unusual finish. Follow the same instructions as for number 1, but as both experience and dexterity are needed in order

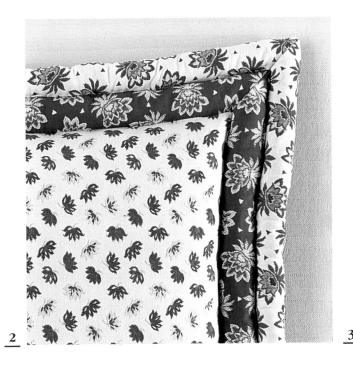

2

3

4

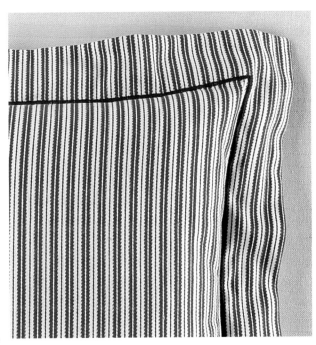

5

to keep the fabrics and corners together neatly, only attempt this if you are sufficiently experienced. Fill and stitch the outer roll in place before the inner one.

3. This contrast border was added without the cushion front or back being piped. Stitch ribbon to each border edge before adding to the cushion front.

4. Another complicated design for the experienced and patient. Make up the cushion front sections at the beginning and pipe. Cut the border pieces over-long, press in half and pin to the cushion. Tack or pin the corners together. Unpin the borders, unfold and stitch across the mitres. Re-pin and make up as the instructions on page 37.

5. The most simple, but nevertheless, extremely effective bordered cushion. Made up as described on page 34, the border is defined by a line of navy blue satin stitch.

OXFORD CUSHIONS

Cushions which are bordered, frilled and buttoned in luxurious cream and white linens, cotton damasks and organdies, sit beautifully together and against the lovely antique French caned headboard.

Cushions are the furnishing accessories which more than anything else can be relied on to change or dictate the style in a room. And making cushions is attractive to almost everyone – experienced makers love to experiment and try new ideas, others cannot resist fabric remnants, scarves and lengths from foreign travel and need to make small items to justify collecting, while those who dislike sewing can almost always be tempted to make some cushions.

Curtains and covers usually need to be started and finished with some urgency, whereas cushions which are smaller and easier to handle can be made over a period of time, either one at a time or picked up and put down as circumstances dictate. Also, for new makers and those who lack confidence, cushions are less threatening and carry the security that should a mistake occur, the cost in terms of both finance and time will not be too great.

Cushions take little fabric, so extravagances can be indulged. If your budget is under pressure it is better by far to economise on the curtain fabrics and to indulge in the accessories: lampshades, tablecloths, screens, footstools and cushions; all of these can show good fabric to its very best advantage. One special cushion placed on a single chair or in the centre of a sofa can entirely alter the perception of the room.

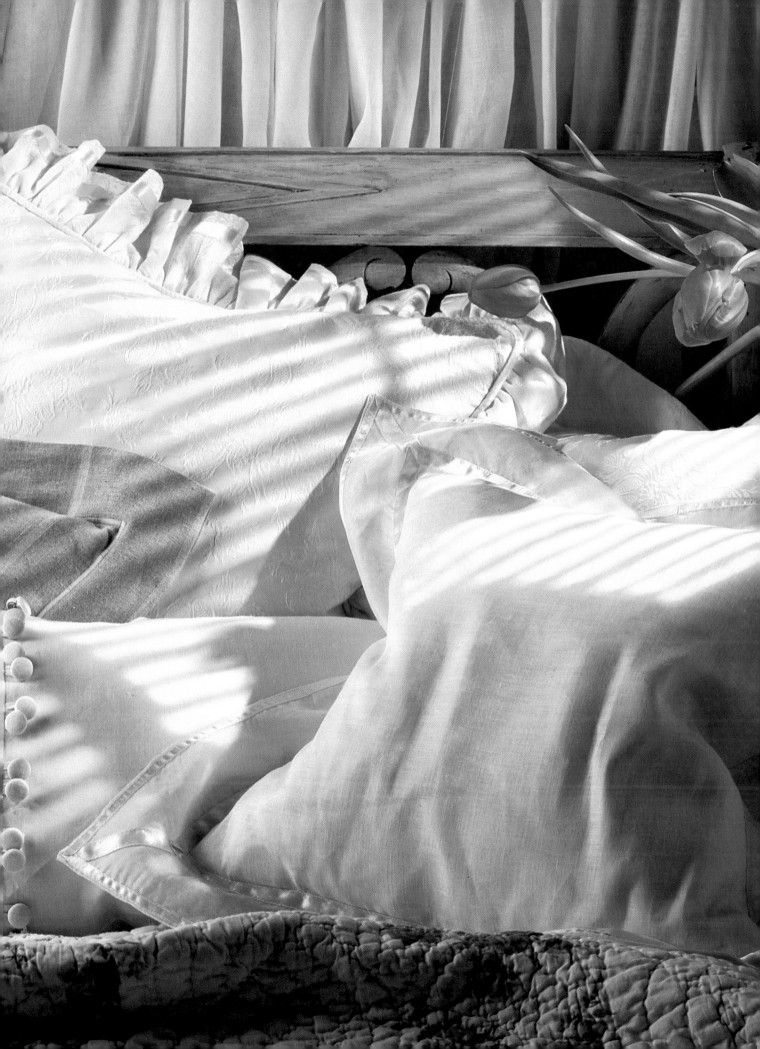

MAKING UP

Add 25 cm (10 in) to the dimensions of the cushion pad (i.e. cut a 70 cm/27½ in) square for a 45 cm/17¾ in square pad). Cut one piece to these measurements for the front and cut one piece the same width but 4 cm (1½ in) longer for the back.

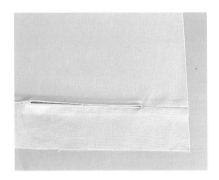

1. Cut 20 cm (8 in) from the back piece. Pin the two pieces together, 2 cm (¾ in) from the raw edges. Stitch 16 cm (6¼ in) in from each side. Press. Insert the zip (page 11) and open it halfway.

Oxford cushions have borders which are folded under to produce two flaps all round (above), whereas a false Oxford cushion has the border made with just one stitching line. It is quite a formal finish, useful in contemporary schemes and with frilled and piped cushions to vary the style.

Linens and cottons in neutral shades have been a favourite for fashion and interior designers for quite some time. This impromptu slipcover (right) was put together in minutes when I found an antique sheet in the cupboard. The look was then completed with cushions in fine woven linens.

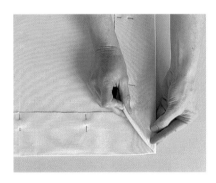

2. Place both pieces on the worktable, with the right sides facing down. Working with each piece consecutively, fold and press over 7 cm (2¾ in). Fold the corners under in turn, to make a false mitre. Pin in place.

3. Place the front piece on to the back piece, with wrong sides together. The corners should align so that each one is folded in the opposite way, and so that they lay flat. Pin all around, 5 cm (2 in) in from the outside edge.

4. Satin stitch all around following the pinned line. The flaps should be free, but firmly stitched, with no raw edges escaping. Open up the zip and fill with the cushion pad.

BOLSTERS

Bolsters have been used as room furnishings long before the arrival of decorative scatter cushions or piles of pillows. Traditionally, bed bolsters were commonly made of straw and stuffed with ferns or horse hair which resulted in a rather firmer pad than our present-day down and feather pillows. Bolsters along the sides of show wood sofas were made for comfort but also for display and, as such, were made from richer fabrics and often trimmed luxuriously. Some early sofas have arms shaped especially to accommodate the side bolsters. Elaborately-embellished bolsters were also made as decoration for day beds.

Bolsters are seeing something of a revival, particularly ornate and decorative versions, which look so well on a sofa or day bed. How you finish the bolster is entirely up to you. Add self-covered buttons, rosettes; finish the ends with soft pleats or tight gathers; use neat piping or a thicker, jumbo cord. Another alternative is simply to tie the 'tail' ends of the bolster in a generous knot or bow (see the red bolster on page 22).

DESIGN AND MAKE CUSHIONS

Making bolsters is a very simple procedure as the centre is always a tube holding the pad. This tube can be plain, assembled from more than one fabric or braided in stripes. The ends can be flat, pleated, ruched, gathered, tied, knotted, buttoned, tasselled, fringed, piped or corded, or almost any form of decoration that you can imagine.

MAKING UP

Measure the space where you plan to site the bolster. Order a feather or down pad approximately 10 per cent larger but make the bolster cover to exactly the length and diameter chosen.

Method 1

1. Cut one piece of fabric the length and circumference of the bolster, adding 2 cm (¾ in) all round for seam allowances. Pin the fabric with right sides together along the length. Stitch 2 cm (¾ in) from the raw edges and 15 cm (6 in) in from each end. Insert the zip as instructed on page 11 or make loops and buttons to close.

2. Cut two circles for the ends, adding 1.5 cm (⅝ in) seam allowance. Make up enough piping or have enough flanged cord to go all round. Pipe around the two circles, snipping often so that the piping lies flat. Stitch in place.

3. Snip around each end at approximately 1.5 cm (⅝ in) intervals and make each cut about 1.5 cm (⅝ in) deep. Pin the right sides to the piping and stitch in place, just inside the piping stitching line. Turn right side out and if any stitching looks uneven, re-stitch until the circle looks perfect.

Method 2

1. Measure the length of the bolster, half way across each end and estimate the length you wish the 'tails' to be. Cut a piece of fabric to this length × the circumference of the bolster, allowing 3 cm (1¼ in) all around for seams.

2. Join the long length with a flat fell seam. Turn under each end by 1.5 cm (⅝ in) twice and hem. Make up ties (page 9), insert the pad and tie the ends.

Method 3

1. Measure, cut and make up the bolster centre piece following step 1 of Method 1. Pipe the two ends following instructions on page 10. Cut sufficient piping to ensure you have only one join at each end.

2. For the two end pieces, cut two stips of fabric to the length of the circumference × the radius of the end plus 1.5 cm (⅝ in) all round for seams. Stitch the short ends together and then stitch one long edge to the centre piece, along the piping line. Turn the raw edge under and hem. Thread a length of cord or tape through. Fill with the pad, pull the tapes tight, knot and stitch to secure. Cover the end with a button, tassel, rosette or other decoration.

A method 1 bolster appears in the main picture on the right, at the top on the right. A bolster made by method 2 is shown on page 22, and a method 3 bolster also appears in the main picture at the bottom on the right.

BOX CUSHIONS

Picnics are one of the eternal joys of summertime and whether at the beach, in the countryside or in your own back garden, what more comfortable way to enjoy the season's fruits than seated on these lovely stencilled box cushions.

A box cushion is one which has a gusset between the top and bottom pieces. So more accurately, they are 'boxed' cushions. Box cushions can be used as scatter cushions, but as the addition of a gusset makes a more bulky cushion, they would either have to be small and decorative to place in front of a larger cushion or on a side chair, or on a very large sofa. Seat cushions for occasional chairs, armchairs, sofas and window seats are always boxed, with fillings of feather and down, firm hair or foam pads depending on personal preference and furniture style.

Duck or goosedown makes the most luxurious and longest lasting cushion filling, but it is also very expensive and can be too soft. A high proportion of feather with some down provides a soft, comfortable and affordable pad. Firm pads can be made traditionally with stitched hair, but more usually from foam covered in a layer of polyester wadding or a quilted feather wrap. See page 14 for more information on fillings.

DESIGN AND MAKE CUSHIONS

MAKING UP

1. Cut out the pieces and make up piping following the instructions on page 10.

2. Place the top and bottom pieces flat on to the worktable, exactly together. Snip irregular marks on all four sides using single, double and triple cuts at 10-20 cm (4-8 in) intervals.

3. Starting on the back edge, pin piping to the right side of the fabric, all round the top and bottom pieces. Pin so that the stitching line will be on the seam allowance. At the corners, snip right up to the stitching line on the piping, open out the cut so that the piping forms a tight corner. Pin securely. Join the piping as instructed on page 10.

4. Stitch on piping. Insert the zip into the gusset strip following the instructions on page 11. Join to the other gusset piece.

5. Starting with the free end of the gusset, pin one side of the gusset to the top of the cover. Match the seam allowance and pin on to the piping line. Cut into the corners, right up to the seam allowance to give a good square corner.

6. Where the zip gusset and the main gusset meet, pin together and stitch the short seam before finishing the pinning. Cut away any excess fabric. Stitch all round as close to the piping as possible. Check from the front that the first piping stitching line is not visible. If it is, stitch around again from the other side, making sure that your stitching line is inside the first one.

7. Pin the other side of the cover to the opposite side of the gusset. Start at the back and, matching the seam allowances, pin along the piping line. Match up the notched marks by scoring a pin line from a notch on the stitched side, across the gusset, following the fabric grain. At each corner score a pin line from the stitched corner to the opposite side of the gusset to align the corners exactly. Snip into the seam allowance. This cut should form the corner. Stitch all around.

8. Cut across the corners to within 5 mm (¼ in) of the stitching. Neaten the seam, open up the zip and turn the cover to the right side. Push each corner to a good shape with a point turner or the end of the scissors. Press all over. Lightly press the seam allowances away from the gusset. Fill the cover with the pad, checking that the filling fits right into each corner.

DESIGN AND MAKE CUSHIONS

Cotton canvas (right) was first washed and stencilled in naive fruit prints, before being made into box cushions with attractive checked fabric gussets piped on the cross.

We have a metal framed pagoda in a sunny corner of our garden (below) which I drape with muslin in the summer. Box cushions make comfortable seating for home picnics and generally lazing around on summer's afternoons. Whether piped or unpiped, stripes and checks should match across the top of back cushions and the front of seat cushions.

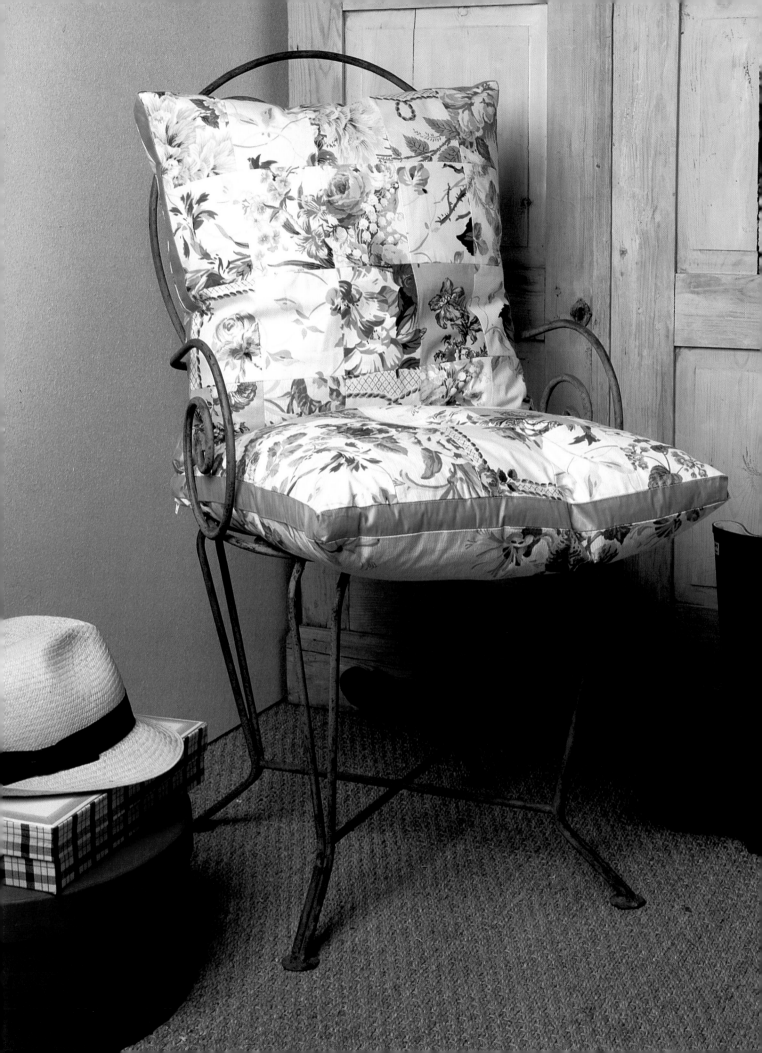

ROUND BOX CUSHIONS

These are made in the same way as any other box cushion, but as the fastening into the gusset is likely to be all too visible, it is usually inserted right across the back.

Take extra care pinning the piping around the circles, snipping the gusset at 1 cm (⅜ in) intervals to prevent the fabric puckering.

The fastening across the back might be a zip or you can experiment with other options, such as buttons with buttonholes or loops.

Make the back in two sections. Cut two half circles and add 4 cm (1½ in) to the width of one and 7 cm (2¾ in) to the other. Make a double turning of 2 cm (¾ in) on both pieces. Place one over the other to form a complete circle and stitch across the join.

Stitch on buttons and buttonholes or tape loops.

I made these cushions to hide an unattractive guest bedroom chair using offcuts from the curtains, the bedcover and the scatter cushions adding just a few other floral chintzes from other rooms. Genuine hand stitched patchwork is a treat to see and to do, but it is not always possible to give the necessary time, so these cut squares were quickly machine stitched, first into lengths and then the lengths into two squares, and made up into box cushions with plain gussets and backs.

SHAPED BOX CUSHIONS

Box cushions for any seat shape are made following the same instructions. See page 12 for measuring and making a template. Lloyd Loom and wicker chairs are shaped around the back.

Box cushions need to be shaped to fit snugly around the arm of a sofa or armchair, into a shaped seat, or on to a shaped stool.

Wicker and garden chairs almost always have seats which are straight along the front and then shaped at the back. Shaped cushions may be turned over so that top and bottom wear equally, but can never be turned back to front, so fastenings must be made into the centre of the gusset. Extend the opening as far around

the shaping as is necessary for the pad to be removed easily. On seat cushions, this will be around the length of the curve. Sofa back cushions will be shaped on one side only and chair cushions on both sides, as they fit around the arms. Open approximately 10 cm (4 in) along a straight side and as far around the arm side as possible without being visible. Never try to make small openings on large covers as heavy pads are very difficult to squeeze in.

TURKISH CORNERS

Turkish style cushions with an over-sized squashy 'piping' are a good alternative to scatter cushions. I make these for very deep sofas and they are also ideal for the person with short legs who has an average depth sofa.

I have to confess, in anticipation of the question, that I have no idea why these cushions are referred to as 'Turkish'. In my mind, I see piles of tasselled cushions in exotic fabrics, elaborately embellished for a bevy of lovely ladies to recline on.

These cushions perform the same function as traditional box cushions but there is no gusset; the top and bottom fabrics are joined along the centre of the cushion side and the corners are pleated or gathered and finished with tassels, knots or buttons.

When I make sofa cushions, I often make traditional boxed corners at the closure end, with the visible corners gathered or pleated in Turkish style. The corners at the back of the cushion will be stitched across at right angles and the excess fabric trimmed away. Plain fabrics with a contrast or toning piping and covered buttons look very stylish and smart, while chintzes and prints look more casual with gathered corners than with bordered box cushions.

MAKING UP

For box Turkish cushions, measure the width and length of the cushion size required and half way down each side, front and back. Add 1.5 cm (⅝ in) all around for seams and cut out front and back pieces.

1. Place the two pieces on to the worktable, right sides together. Snip through both layers at random intervals, two or three times along each side. I always prefer to fit these cushion to the pad so that I know the corners will fit perfectly. So, lay both pieces over the top and bottom of the cushion pad and pin together all around, gathering or pleating the corners to fit tightly. Trim away any excess fabric at the corners, and mark with coloured tacks so that the two pieces will fit together again exactly.

2. Make up piping and stitch to the top piece all round, pleating or gathering corners as marked. Stitch in place.

3. Place the two pieces together and pin around the back corners. Stitch 3 cm (1¼ in) from each end and insert the zip, following the instructions on page 11. Open up the zip halfway.

4. Pin the back to the front along the piping line, matching the corners and the snipped markers. Stitch close to the piping inside the first stitching line. Turn to the front and check that the piping is even. If not, re-stitch.

Turkish corners make an ideal finish for large seat cushions (right), without the formal lines of a box cushion. The crisp cottons in bold, spring colours of yellow and blue and the complementary fabric designs are used throughout the room. The seat cushions are piped in strong turquoise to give a defining edge, and make a strong statement of contrast. This effect is echoed in the piping of the scatter cushions.

Pleated corners are a more formal finish on Turkish cushions and usually only used for sofa, chair or floor cushions. The self-covered button (below) adds an understated finish. These cushions can make a small pile to be used for an extra seat or side table. The same fabric with fuller, softer pads, decorated with elaborate gold tassels, would make plump, casual floor cushions.

TIED CUSHION COVERS

Wrapping a cover over a seat cushion to tie at the front is the most stylish solution to a common practical problem that I have found. Sofa and chair covers are always difficult to keep clean, truly washable fabrics are limited and light colours easily marked however careful you are.

I work often in country homes where the requirements of outdoor life play an important part in our choice of fabrics and colours, at least for the family rooms. Gardeners, farmers, hunters and walkers all prefer to flop into the nearest sofa or chair with little thought of removing muddy clothing.

Preventing children from climbing on to furniture with shoes on and sticky biscuits in hand is also virtually impossible, and even the most washable slip cover takes considerable time to launder well.

An over-cover which is no more than a square of fabric with added ties may be washed and replaced as often as is needed.

Covers tied over cushions (above right) do have a practical aspect but are mainly chosen for decoration.

Seat cushions furnished with tied over-covers (right) are an attractive and functional option.

DESIGN AND MAKE CUSHIONS

Stripes and checks in similar colourings are old favourites for country schemes. Striped over cushions can be made up on three sides and hemmed open along the fourth to reveal unpiped under-cushions in toning checks. Attach tapes, ribbons or self fabric ties cut on the straight or on the cross to bring together the open edges. Experiment with other combinations and ideas. Cover summer chintz cushions with tartan winter over covers, or make checked floor cushions for children's rooms with appliquéd over covers.

Pinky red denim squares (left) were first hemmed all round and then eyelets were made in each corner. Eyelet kits are readily available from ships' chandlers and hardware stores, but if you like the idea but are unable to find eyelets, cut holes and blanket stitch around in a contrast coloured thread. Ties in the same fabric as the unpiped under-cushion are pulled through and tied to hold the two squares together. Make the squares approximately 15 per cent smaller than the under-cushion or they will keep slipping off.

Little more than a square of fabric, an over cover can create a really pleasing effect (above). Measure across the cushion to find the side length for the covers. Over cut by 2 cm (¾ in) all round and hem each side. Make ties following instructions on page 9 and stitch to each corner. Tie the back and front pieces together, tightly enough to keep the cover in place but not to squash the under-cushion.

Tied striped over covers have been made to slip over simple, checked scatter cushions in toning shades of blue and cream.

FINISHES AND FABRICS

With the addition of a simple plain border, this beautiful piece of crewel work has been transformed into an exquisite scatter cushion for the study.

Inspiration for cushion making and styles can come from a wide variety of sources. Fabulous pieces of antique needlework or old fabrics can be incorporated into new cushions with a minimum of work. Samples of needlepoint can be used as central panels for cushions, or they can form a border to another fabric. If you enjoy traditional needlework, embroidery or other hand stitching, try to include these skills in your cushions. Pintucks make delightful finishing touches, as do buttons, ties and appliqué. Cushions need not be permanent fixtures as say a chair cover or curtains. Consider making cushion covers in fresh stripes and floral prints for the summer months, slipping on covers of damasks, tweeds and wools for the winter. Treat yourself to a few special silk and taffeta covers kept for special dinner parties and quickly stencil a simple Christmas or birthday motif on to calico for a family party.

Dress and evening wear fabrics, in wonderfully rich and lush colours, textures, prints and weaves are often more reasonably priced than curtain fabrics, and although they will not last as long, can be used to create many and varied cushion designs, especially for seasonal or occasional use.

NEEDLEPOINT

Needlepoint has always been a popular pastime, canvases often being stitched to be used as sofa cushions. Once the canvas has been successfully stretched, make it into piped or frilled cushions following instructions on pages 22 and 26, mount on to fabric, or frame with fabric borders.

I was given the two antique workings (shown left) and asked to make them into cushions for this kelim-covered sofa. I chose tightly woven cotton velvet for its rich soft texture which contrasts so wonderfully with the rough wool kelim. Neither of the colours exactly matches any in the kelim but both were selected for their aged tones which blend beautifully.

Both pieces were made into box cushions with narrow piped gussets – the larger floral pattern bordered with rich terracotta velvet and the round cushion framed with ruched velvet.

I bought the wool chain-stitched crewel works (featured on page 59) with the intention of covering two chair seats, but decided instead to make them into scatter cushions for the study. A simply made border in a plain fabric picks out one of the colours and frames the work.

I made these two antique workings into box cushions with narrow piped gussets for this kelim-covered sofa (left). The square cushion is bordered with rich terracotta velvet and the round cushion framed with ruched velvet.

Cut four strips of fabric approximately 7 cm (2¾ in) wide × 14 cm (5½ in) longer than the work. Stitch each border to one side of the work in turn, with 1.5 cm (⅝ in) seam allowances and leaving the last 7 cm (2¾ in) of each piece free. Stitch the free pieces to each other along the short ends. Make up as a basic piped or unpiped cushion following the instructions on pages 18 or 24.

Beautiful, handmade tassels (left) have been stitched to the corners of this crewel work cusion, seen in full on page 59. The colours in the tassel pick up the various threads of the needlework.

The subtly coloured tartan print (below) harmonises with all of the colours used in the work and the wide border has been quilted for fun. Follow the instructions on page 42 to make up an Oxford cushion, quilting each piece before making it up and using cotton cord instead of a piped edge.

BUTTONS AND HAND STITCHING

Buttons as fastenings are infinitely more attractive (right) than present-day zippers. Machine-stitched button holes are perfectly satisfactory, but make hand sewn buttonholes for a really professional finish. If you are already *au fait* with hand stitching your buttonholes you will know how little effort is required for a very satisfying result. In any case, do take the plunge and make your fastening a feature on the front of the cushion.

PINTUCKS

Traditional dressmaking finishes and hand stitching are gradually being revived and re-introduced to soft furnishings by interior designers.

Pintucks are one of the most straightforward and adaptable of finishes. Fold tucks accurately and stitch with small machine or neat hand stitches.

Stitching pintucks together to form their own design is just one way to vary the traditional format. Keep main fabric, tucks and thread in tones of the same colour for a sophisticated look or match the thread to the main fabric with contrast tucks for a striking effect.

MAKING UP

Make a template of the cushion front in calico or scrap fabric, pinning rows of tucks in position as you wish, adjusting the amount and size until you are satisfied. Use the final template to cut the cushion front. Cut the back piece to the size of the pad plus 1.5 cm (⅝ in) seam allowance.

1. If the pintucks are to be in a contrasting fabric, cut the main fabric into strips and stitch sections in to correspond with the number and width of tucks. Press along the centre of the first tuck and pin fabrics together at right angles to the tuck. Using the machine foot guide for accuracy, stitch along the length of the tuck, parallel to the folded line. Repeat with the other tucks. Press and make up the cushion cover following the instructions on page 18.

2. For self-fabric tucks, plan the stitched design on the template and mark each tuck accordingly with fine pencil or marking tacks. Hand stitch tucks together with embroidery thread. Press and make up the cushion cover following the instructions on page 18.

Buttons provide a practical and decorative fastening to these linen scatter cushions. Choose buttons to complement the cushion fabric and room setting.

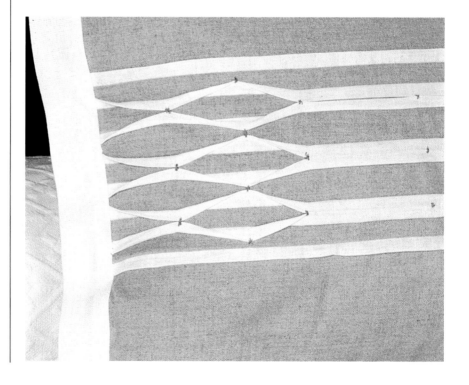

DESIGN AND MAKE CUSHIONS

BORDERS AND BUTTONS

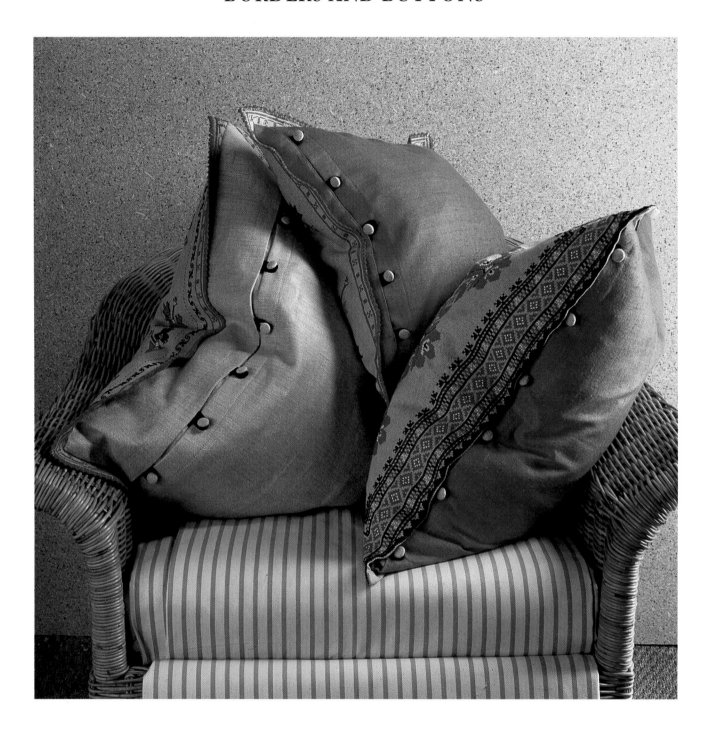

A friend brought these incredibly beautifully hand stitched panels back from Bulgaria and asked me to make them into cushions. As the backs should always be in the same fabric, we used linen weave silks. Covered buttons and ribbon loops echo the thread colours and are as beautifully crafted as the fronts.

DESIGN AND MAKE CUSHIONS

Purely decorative, pintucks can be as subtle as you wish: tiny tucks in neat rows giving a delicate air to fine cotton or linen; or deliberately striking: deeper tucks across the whole cushion, each in a different colour.

Rouleau loops and tiny fabric covered buttons do not just belong on wedding dresses and couture gowns. Fine woven fabrics make the best loops – use cotton, silk or linen.

USING STRIPES

Striped fabrics perhaps present the greatest challenge to all makers who like to experiment and to make something different each time. I used cotton denim in a deep green for the backs to tone with the green stripes and for Oxford cushions to temper the vibrancy of the multi-directional stripes.

For all of the cushion fronts, first cut a template the size of the pad, from calico or spare fabric. Mark out into sections as shown. Mark the direction of the stripes in pencil. Place these pieces on to

the main fabric, checking that the stripes are running as planned. Cut around the pattern pieces, adding 1.5 cm (⅝ in) seam allowance to each side.

1. Divide the cushion front into three equal sections and cut out across the grain. Join so that the stripes zigzag across the cushion.
2. Mark out with a centre square sitting diagonally over straight stripes.
3. Divide the template from corner to corner to produce four triangles. Join in pairs to make two triangles and then to make the square. The centre and

diagonals must match exactly.
4. Cut the whole front on the cross and stitch the border with the deepest coloured thread.
5. Divide the template from corner to corner into four small triangles. Position on the main fabric very carefully to make quite sure that the centres will match and the stripes remain true.
6. Draw a square over the top and cut the template into five pieces. Place the border pieces together as you cut to make sure that the corners are kept at 45°. These cushions are great fun for children's rooms, garden rooms, summerhouses or outdoors.

DESIGN AND MAKE CUSHIONS

1

2

3

4

5

6

WINDOW SEATS AND SETTLES

My kitchen has a deep sill overlooking a courtyard which has become the first place everyone chooses to sit since I made a squashy feather and down seat.

Window seats can be the deep sills of low recessed windows or they may be fitted into a bay below the sill. Often there is a radiator underneath, but if not, the seat can be made to lift and the area beneath used for storage. In a deep recess, back cushions or scatter cushions can be added. Children love to curl up and read in a comfortable, secure window seat, and most of us like to sit with a drink looking out of the window.

A similar proposition for the cushion maker is the antique wooden sofa or settle which would be much too uncomfortable to use for relaxing, but which fits well into hallways and kitchens. These pieces of furniture ask for cushions to cover their seats and backs to soften and make them more welcoming.

Cushion covers and pads for both window seats and wooden settles or sofas need to be made with a soft filling if they are to be comfortable to sit on. Traditionally, straw or horse hair was stitched tightly into seat pads covered with cotton covers, but these are too hard for today's more comfortable lifestyle and so a variety of standard cushion fillings to suit varying needs has been adapted and these are readily available.

Feather and down mixes make comfortable, squashy pads, foam pads are firm but not too comfortable, while a compromise might be a foam pad covered with fibre or feather wrap. If you prefer to use a firmer pad, keep the gusset narrow and button through following the instructions on page 74.

DESIGN AND MAKE CUSHIONS

MAKING A SEAT CUSHION

Estimate the amount of fabric you will need by measuring the longest and widest point of the seat. Add a 4 cm (1½ in) seam allowance in each direction. Measure for the gusset 10 cm (4 in) from the back of the pad along one side, across the front and along the other side to 10 cm (4 in) from the back. Add 2 cm (5 in) either side of the width for seam allowance, and 4 cm (1½ in) to the length.

A suitable border printed with the main fabric is a bonus if there is a window seat to be made (left). The skirt is purely decorative, made up separately and attached to the seat rather than made up with the pad cover. A flat band fitted with press stud tape to the front of the seat holds the gathered skirt in place.

An ugly radiator needed to be covered up (right) but without any substantial heat loss. The sill was not deep enough to be a comfortable seat but still needed to be covered so that the skirt would look right. The top was cut as for a window seat, quilted, and piped. The skirt was made with a length of fabric lined and box pleated to fit the width of the seat and stitched to the piping line. The top was then lined and slip stitched over all the raw edges to neaten them.

The rest of the gusset will need to be cut in two pieces so that the zip can be inserted along the centre. Cut two strips the length of the remaining gusset plus 4 cm (1½ in) for seam allowance and two strips the width of the gusset plus 2 cm (¾ in) allowance for the zip and 2 cm (¾ in) for the seam on each piece.

Plan these pieces (top, bottom, gusset, piping) on the worktable to see how they fit into the fabric width. If you are making several cushions which go together they must be planned for maximum benefit from the fabric.

If the fabric has a dominant pattern, the template will need to be planned so that the cushions are cut together to prevent wastage of fabric.

If possible make the cushion covers reversible.

The pattern should read from front to back. The gusset should be cut so that the pattern follows through and matched to either side of the piping.

Make up window seat cushions using the suggestions for fillings on page 14 and following the instructions for box cushions on page 48.

SQUAB SEAT CUSHIONS

Kitchen chairs are made to be easily moveable and practical to clean, are often wooden or wooden with rush or caned seats but can rarely be described as comfortable. Metal chairs, although decorative, are only designed for short term comfort. However, piped squab cushions make even the most uncomfortable wooden or metal seats pleasing to sit on.

MAKING UP

Make a template of the chair seat and buy or make a cushion pad as described on page 15.

1. Cut two pieces for the top and bottom allowing the depth of the seat pad and 2 cm (¾ in) seam allowance all around, place together and cut balance marks on each side to help re-matching later.

2. Make up enough piping to go around the squab, (or use flanged cord). Pin the piping all round the bottom piece on the right side of the fabric. The piping stitching line should be on the seam allowance, raw edges matching. Snip at regular intervals to keep the piping flat, fold tight into the corners and join, following the instructions on page 10.

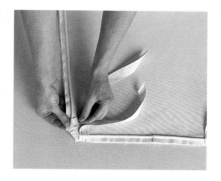

3. Make up ties and pin to the piping line, positioned to either side of the chair legs. Stitch to the seam several times. These ties will take a lot of strain, so strengthening them now could save a lot of irritation and fiddly repairs later.

4. Pin the front and back piece right sides together between the back legs. Stitch for 2–3 cm (¾–1¼ in) from either side, close to the piping. Insert the zip, following the instructions on page 11. Open up the zip and pin around the other three sides. Match notches exactly. Stitch close to the piping, inside the piping stitching line.

5. Snip into the corners, turn to the right side and check that the piping is stitched tightly and evenly. If not, stitch around again, pushing the machine foot close to the piping cord. Neaten the seam and turn right sides out.

Shaping

Some squab seats have quite complicated shaping around either the back or the front legs. Cut the fabric to your template and snip and bend piping so that it lies flat. You might prefer to choose a finer but tightly woven fabric for the piping so that it is easier to handle.

Use feather filled pads for a soft, informal look or foam or hair pads for a more solid looking seat. For a country kitchen or bedroom chair, add a frilled or straight skirt at the end of step 2, finishing at either side of the legs.

An elegant piped squab seat cushion with sash ties was quite straight-forward to make and adds comfort and discreet decoration to this rather formal metal chair.

BUTTONING

1. Either mark the template with the button positions or place buttons on to the pad and pin in place. Measure the distances between each button point and mark with a soft pencil or vanishing pen. These marks will be covered by the buttons. If you are as yet unsure of the position, use crossed pins. Mark exactly the same positions on the bottom piece.

2. Using heavy duty thread and a strong needle, push through from the underside to the top. Thread through a button and knot. Push the needle back through to within 4 mm (¼ in) of the first hole. Thread through the button or straight into the underside, and pull the threads tightly to give a slight indentation in the pad. Knot three times and cut threads.

Cleaning

If the squab is for occasional use and unlikely to be cleaned often, omit the zip and slip stitch the opening closed by hand.

To clean the squab, cut the threads, remove the cover and launder according to the type of fabric and fillings used. Replace the buttons when clean and dry.

Contrast piping and buttoning make a boxed squab very striking and suitable for the most formal of rooms. Period dining chairs often have caned seats which need squab cushions for comfort. Traditional damasks and brocades or simple woven stripes all benefit from piping and buttoning.

CHAIR
LEG TIES

Squab cushions need to be
securely fixed to the back legs of
your chair. Ties should be stitched
very firmly to the seam inside and
long enough to tie or button
tightly without allowing too much
movement.

Box squab cushions are deeper
than piped squabs so are suitable
for dining chairs and can give
some height to chairs which are
slightly too low for comfort.

Make the seat template and pad
as before, fit the zip between the
back chair legs and stitch ties
between the gusset, but make up
following the instructions for box
cushions on page 48.

1. Knotted ribbon ends hold a
single bead in place. Gilded or
pearl drops, multicoloured or
wooden beads would make
equally effective decorations used
singly or in long rows.
2. Stitch buttons and make
buttonholes into petersham ribbon
or self ties for a smart finish.
3. Petersham or double-sided satin
ribbon is tied in decorative bows
which also holds the pad to the
chair seat. Use gingham ribbon or
woven Tyrolean braid for
children's and kitchen chair seats.
4. Make rouleau or folded ties from
the main cushion or piping fabric
or use ribbon, cotton or petersham
which performs the same function.
Strap around the chair leg to hold
the pad in place and decorate the
leg at the same time.

STOOL CUSHIONS

I have made many of these squashy fabric stools for bathrooms, nurseries and children's bedrooms. Very sophisticated, luxurious models in blue and navy velvet, simpler black and white stripes, elegant cream and coffee canvas, country floribunda roses, rich tartans and paisleys are some of the fabrics and combinations which have been used to great effect in different settings.

Decide the diameter and height which you need, divide the circumference into six and cut six rectangular sections. Stitch together with piping or cord to join, hem top and bottom and gather up with a drawstring. Make the top with heavy buckram or card covered in foam and polyester wadding. Pipe all around and handstitch into the gathered top. Fill with beans or a large feather pad.

An exotic crimson and gold fabric has been made into an opulent stool cushion, perfect for an intimate corner.

Box and Turkish cushions make comfortable seats for wooden or metal stools. Use plain or self fabric tapes to hold the cushion to the stool. Pin to the bottom of the cushion cover before the gusset is stitched in place. If you have ties at the corners, fit one tape to each side of the corner and tie underneath. Determine the size of the piping to complement the pad design.

1. Vary the basic box cushion by sectioning the top into four triangles. Emphasise with black piping and finish with a self covered button.

2. Sash width ties stitched into the gusset corners tie into bows or knots, and hide the fixing tapes holding the cushion to the stool.

3. A skirt, made up and stitched to the underside of the cover before the gusset is stitched around can be used to cover any sort of damage to an old stool or chair seat, but here it has been used purely for decoration. The gentle, piped scallops take nothing away from the shape or line of the stool.

4. Ties stitched into the gusset corners can be tied as a bow or knotted, hiding the corner fixing tapes. Self piping on the cross gives a good finish. Here, chunky piping cord has been used to make the pad look deeper than it really is.

5. Centre piped, Turkish style cushions are less formal than box cushions. Long sash ties cut in one piece with the top and bottom, knot and drape extravagantly down the leg of the chair.

DESIGN AND MAKE CUSHIONS

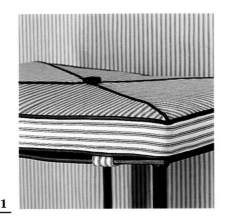

1

2

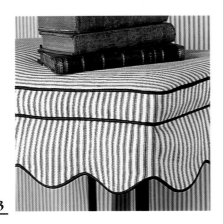

3

4

5

GLOSSARY

FIBRES

Acrylic Manmade from petrol, often mixed with more expensive fibres to keep the cost down. Not hardwearing, but useful for permanent pleating.

Cotton A natural fibre, cotton is very versatile, woven, knitted and mixed with other fibres. Used for any soft furnishings according to weight. It will lose strength in direct sunlight, so protect. Soft, strong, easy to launder, washable if pre-shrunk.

Linen Fibres found inside the stalks of the flax plant are woven to make linen cloth in almost any weight. Distinctive slub weave from very fine linen for under-curtains and sheers to heavy upholstery weight. A very strong fibre which is easy to work and will take high temperatures.

Silk From the cocoon of the silk worm, silk is soft and luxurious to touch. Fades in sunlight, so protect. Available in every weight, suitable for soft furnishings, from lampshades to heavy upholstery. Good mixed with cotton or wool.

Wool A natural fibre, liable to excessive shrinkage as the 'scales' on each fibre overlap, harden and 'felt'. Is warm to touch and initially resists damp. Ideal for upholstery and curtains.

Viscose Wood pulp woven into fibres which mixes well with other fibres helping them to take dyes and fireproofing. Washable and sheds dirt easily.

FABRICS

Brocade Traditionally woven fabric using silk, cotton, wool or mixed fibres, on a jacquard loom, in a multi or self coloured floral design. Brocades drape well and can be used for curtains, traditional bed drapes, covers and upholstery. Some are washable but most will need dry cleaning.

Calico Coarse, plain weave cotton in cream or white with 'natural' flecks in it. Available in many widths and weights for inexpensive curtains, bed drapes, garden awnings. Wash before use to shrink and press while damp.

Cambric Closely woven, plain weave fabric from linen or cotton with a sheen on one side. Use, wash and press as Calico. Widely used for cushion pad covers but also for curtains, covers and cushions.

Canvas Plain weave cotton in various weights suitable for upholstered chair covers, inexpensive curtains, slip covers, awnings and outdoor use. Available as unbleached, coarse cotton or more finely woven and dyed in strong colours.

Chintz Cotton fabric with Eastern design using flowers and birds, often with a resin finish which gives a characteristic sheen or glaze and which also repels dirt. The glaze will eventually wash out, so only dry clean curtains. Avoid using steam to press and never fold or the glaze will crack.

Corduroy A strong fabric woven to form vertical ribs by floating extra yarn across which is then cut to make the pile. Use for traditional upholstery. Press on a velvet pinboard while damp.

Crewel Plain or hopsack woven, natural cotton background embroidered in chain stitch in plain cream wool or multi-coloured wools. Soft but heavy, lovely for curtains, soft blinds, cushions and light-use loose covers. May be washed, but test a small piece first.

Damask A jacquard fabric first woven in Damascus with satin floats on a warp satin background in cotton, silk, wool and mixed fibres in various weights. Use for curtains, drapes and sometimes covers and upholstery, choosing different weights for different uses. Make up reversed if a matt finish is required. Suitable for curtaining which needs to be seen from both sides.

Gingham Plain weave fabric with equal width stripes of white plus one other colour in both warp and weft threads to produce blocks of checks or stripes in 100% cotton. Use for small windows in cottagey rooms, kitchens, children's bedrooms and slip covers. Mix with floral patterns and other checks and stripes.

Holland Firm, hardwearing fabric made from cotton or linen stiffened with oil or shellac. Used for blinds lightweight covers, curtaining and pelmets.

Lace Open work fabrics in designs ranging from simple spots to elaborate panels. Usually in cotton or a cotton and polyester mixture.

Moiré A finish usually on silk or acetate described as 'watermarked'. The characteristic moiré markings are produced by pressing plain woven fabric through hot engraved cylinders which crush the threads and push them into different directions to form the pattern. This finish will disappear on contact with water, so it is not suitable for upholstery.

Muslin White or off-white, inexpensive, open-weave cloth which can be dyed in pastel colours. Used for under-curtains and sheers in hot countries to filter light and insects.

Organdie The very finest cotton fabric with an acid finish giving it a unique crispness. Use for lightweight curtains, dressing tables and lampshades. Wash and press while damp.

Organza Similar to organdie and made of silk, polyester or viscose. Very springy and used for stiffening headings of fine fabrics, blinds to filter sunlight and to protect curtains. Use layers of varying tones or pastel colours over each other.

Provençal prints Small print designs printed by hand on to fine cotton for curtains, upholstery, cushions and covers. Washable, hard wearing, soft and easy to work with.

Silk noil Light to mediumweight silk, relatively inexpensive for interlining heavy curtains, slip covers, summer curtains and cushions.

Silk shantung Light to mediumweight silk woven with irregular yarns giving a dull, rough appearance. Use for curtains, cushions, light drapes and lampshades. Available in an extensive range of colours, gathers and frills.

Taffeta Woven from silk, acetate and blends. Used for elaborate drapes because it handles well and for its light-reflecting qualities.

Tartan Authentic tartans belong to individual Scottish clans and are of woven or worsted fine twill weave with an elaborate checked design. Traditional wool tartans are hardwearing for upholstering sofas and chairs, curtains and cushions.

Ticking Characteristic original herringbone weave in black and white, now woven in many colours and weights. Use for curtains and upholstery. Not usually pre-shrunk.

Toile de jouy Pastoral designs in one colour printed on to calico using copper plate printing techniques. Use for curtains, covers, upholstery, cushions and bedding.

Tweed Wool or worsted cloth in square or rectangular checked designs in few colours. Often used for shawls or more tightly woven for men's sporting clothes. However, use for upholstering stools, chairs, sofas or for curtains, pelmets and cushions.

Velvet Originally 100% silk, now made from cotton, viscose or other manmade fibres. Woven with a warp pile and additional yarn in loops which are up to 3 mm (⅛ in) depth to form a pile. Care needs to be taken when sewing or the fabrics will 'walk'. Press on a velvet pinboard. Dry clean carefully. Always buy good quality velvet with a dense pile which will not pull out easily.

Voile Fine, light plain weave cotton or polyester fabric dyed in many plain colours. Use for filmy curtains, bed drapes and under-curtains. Easily washable and little pressing necessary. Silk and wool voiles can be used for fine drapery.

CARE FOR CUSHIONS

Cushions perform many different functions within the home and you will already have chosen fabrics suitable for the purpose.

Test a piece of fabric first for shrinkage and decide whether to wash before making up or to allow the shrinkage allowance.

It is always advisable to choose washable fabrics for cushions which will be in constant use – especially window seats and those used as scatter or floor cushions.

Remove dust from scatter cushions, window seats and sofa cushions daily. Really bash the pad from each side between your fists or drop each cushion on to the floor one corner at a time to knock air back in, dust out, and the feathers back into the corners.

Decorative cushions from occasional chairs, drawing rooms and bedrooms are likely to be made from more delicate fabrics or at least with decorative detail which might need special care.

The very best way to care for these cushions is to make sure that they never need to be washed or dry cleaned. Regular dusting with a clean soft cloth, and occasional vacuuming with a soft brush covered with a muslin cap will keep cushions clean. Hang cushions in a cotton bag outside on a warm spring day with a light breeze to freshen fabrics and feather pads.

Many home care kits are available for specific stains and can be used successfully on most fabrics.

INDEX